T0407310

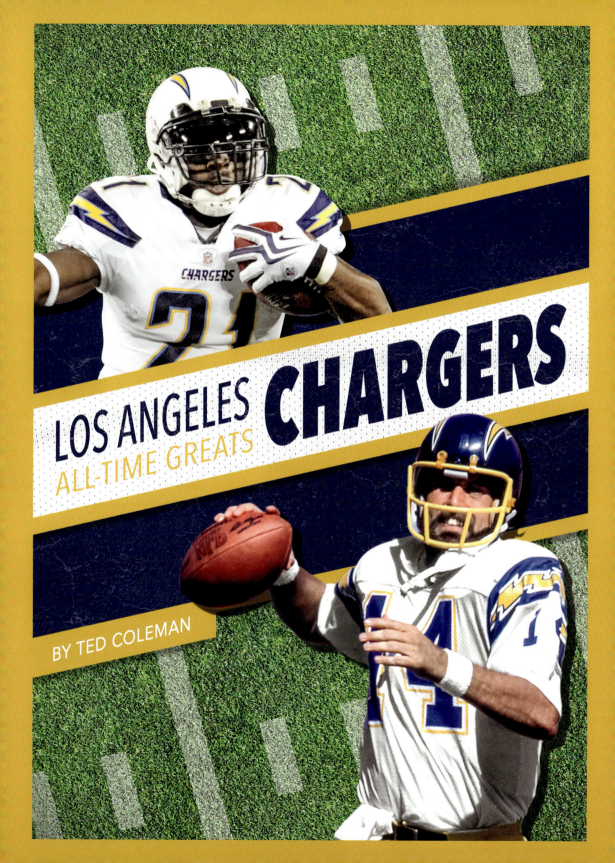

LOS ANGELES CHARGERS

ALL-TIME GREATS

BY TED COLEMAN

Book design by Jake Slavik
Cover design by Jake Slavik

Photographs ©: John Russell/AP Images, cover (top), 1 (top); Tony Tomsic/AP Images, cover (bottom), 1 (bottom); James Flores/Getty Images Sport/Getty Images, 4; Focus on Sport/Getty Images, 7; Dennis Desprois/Getty Images Sport/Getty Images, 8; Tony Duffy/Allsport/Hulton Archive/Getty Images, 10; Andy Hayt/Sports Illustrated/Getty Images, 13; Scott Quintard/Getty Images Sport/Getty Images, 14; Robert B. Stanton/NFL Photo Library/Getty Images Sport/Getty Images, 17; Donald Miralle/Getty Images Sport/Getty Images, 19; Wesley Hitt/Getty Images Sport/Getty Images, 21

Press Box Books, an imprint of Press Room Editions.

ISBN
978-1-63494-429-8 (library bound)
978-1-63494-446-5 (paperback)
978-1-63494-479-3 (epub)
978-1-63494-463-2 (hosted ebook)

Library of Congress Control Number: 2021916621

Distributed by North Star Editions, Inc.
2297 Waters Drive
Mendota Heights, MN 55120
www.northstareditions.com

Printed in the United States of America
012022

ABOUT THE AUTHOR

Ted Coleman is a sportswriter who lives in Louisville, Kentucky, with his trusty Affenpinscher, Chloe.

TABLE OF CONTENTS

HADL
21

CHAPTER 1
AFL GLORY YEARS

The Los Angeles Chargers played their first season in 1960. At the time, they were members of the brand-new American Football League (AFL). The Chargers didn't stay in Los Angeles for long, though. In 1961, the team moved south to San Diego. Two years later, they won the AFL championship. The Chargers crushed the Boston Patriots 51–10 in the title game. Veteran quarterback **Tobin Rote** led the way. He tossed two touchdown passes in the game. Backup quarterback **John Hadl** got some playing time at the end of the game. He went on to lead the Chargers for the next nine seasons. In his 11 years with the team, Hadl threw for 26,938 yards and 201 touchdowns.

Hadl succeeded with the help of a strong offensive line. Right tackle **Ron Mix** was one of the greatest linemen of the 1960s. His outstanding blocking earned him a spot in the Hall of Fame. Meanwhile, right guard **Walt Sweeney** was as reliable as they came. In his 11 seasons with the Chargers, he didn't miss a single game.

FEARSOME FOURSOME

In the early 1960s, San Diego's defensive line was known as the Fearsome Foursome. And there was plenty for opposing teams to be afraid of. The four defenders had an average height of 6-foot-6. Their average weight was 270 pounds. The group included Earl Faison, Ernie Ladd, Bill Hudson, and Ron Nery. Faison and Ladd were both members of the 1963 championship team.

ALWORTH
19

Hadl also had a top target in wide receiver **Lance Alworth**. Alworth's amazing catches and graceful running style thrilled fans. He scored 83 touchdowns during his nine years with the team. Alworth stayed with the Chargers until 1970. That was when the AFL merged with the National Football League (NFL).

CHAPTER 2
AIR CORYELL

In the late 1970s and early 1980s, **Fred Dean** led San Diego's defense. Dean was a strong and fast pass rusher. He recorded 52 sacks as a Charger. However, that number is unofficial. That's because sacks weren't an official stat until 1982. Even so, Dean had a huge impact on the team's defense.

As great as Dean was, the Chargers were all about offense. Head coach Don Coryell built his offense around the passing game. Quarterback **Dan Fouts** put up numbers that had never been seen before. From 1979 to 1981, he had three 4,000-yard passing seasons

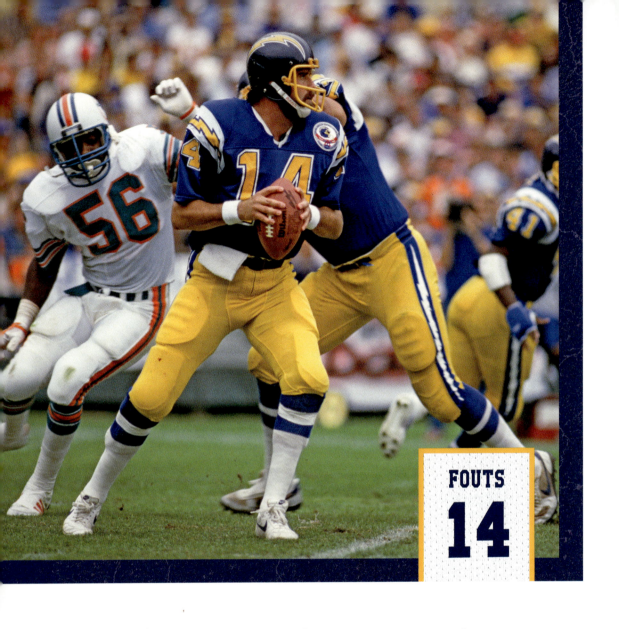

FOUTS

14

in a row. Fouts was the first player in NFL history to achieve that. He was also just the third quarterback to record 40,000 career passing yards. Opposing teams knew that Fouts wasn't a mobile quarterback. But they still couldn't stop him from picking their defenses apart.

It helped that Fouts had several stars to throw to. **Charlie Joiner** was a speedy receiver with excellent hands. He spent 11 years with the Chargers. During that time, he racked up 9,203 receiving yards. When Joiner retired, he had more catches than anyone in league history.

Receiver **Wes Chandler** was another of Fouts's favorite targets. Chandler had one of his best seasons in 1982. He averaged 129 yards per game that year. That was still an NFL record as of 2021.

STAT SPOTLIGHT

PASSING YARDS IN A SEASON
CHARGERS TEAM RECORD
Dan Fouts: 4,802 (1981)

Kellen Winslow helped change the entire position of tight end. Tight ends usually had the job of blocking or catching short passes. Winslow was certainly big enough to block. But he had the speed and catching ability of a receiver. That made him very difficult to defend. Injuries shortened his career. However, he still managed to rack up 6,741 receiving yards and 45 touchdowns.

Fouts couldn't have made so many passes without a great offensive line. Right tackle **Russ Washington** helped keep defenders away from Fouts. He earned a

DON CORYELL

Don Coryell was the head coach for San Diego State University from 1961 to 1972. That's when he began designing his passing offense. He had perfected it by the time he became the Chargers' head coach in 1978. His offense became known as "Air Coryell." San Diego led the league in passing each year from 1978 to 1983.

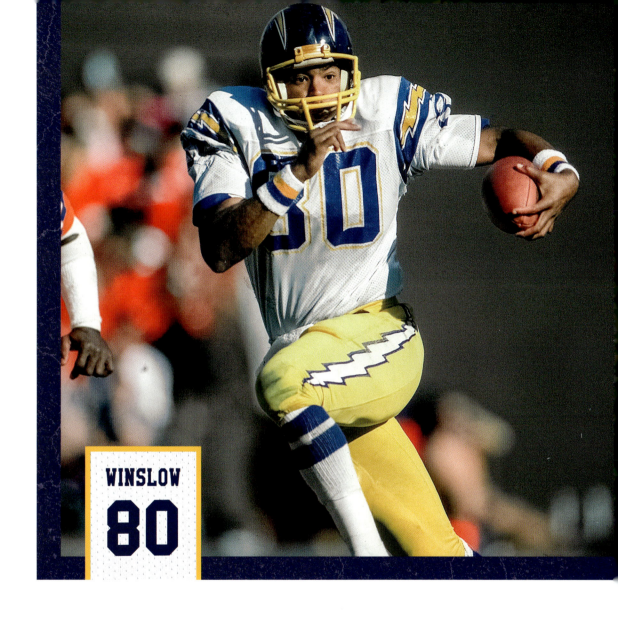

WINSLOW
80

trip to five Pro Bowls during his long career with the Chargers. Meanwhile, **Doug Wilkerson** was a dependable left guard. He appeared in three Pro Bowls.

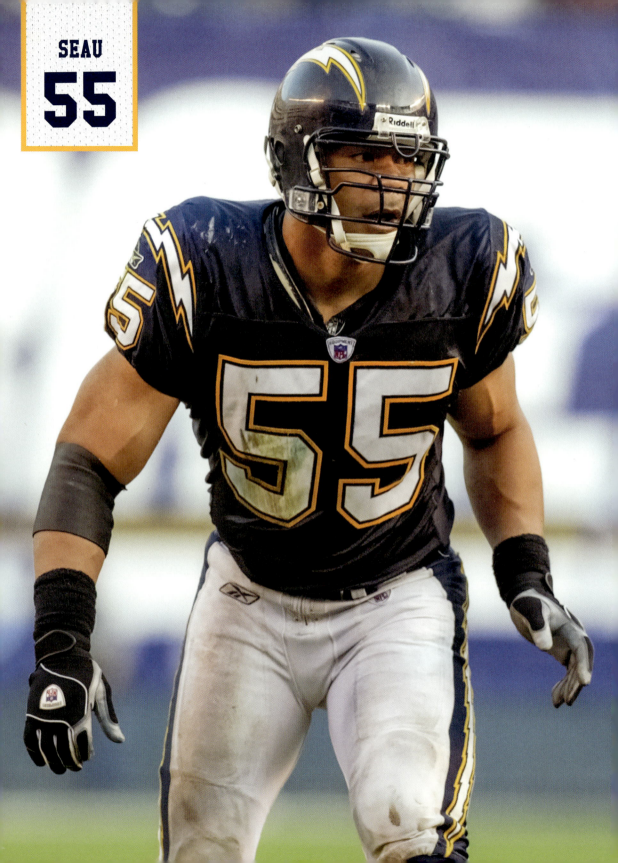

SEAU

55

CHAPTER 3
SUPER CHARGERS

Even with all that talent, the "Air Coryell" Chargers never made it to the Super Bowl. The team that did came as a total surprise. The 1994 Chargers were led by defensive players like **Leslie O'Neal**. The star defensive end was an outstanding pass rusher. He went on to become the team's all-time leader in sacks.

Few players had a bigger impact on the Chargers than linebacker **Junior Seau**. Seau was a native of the San Diego area. Teammates loved his leadership and hard work. Fans loved his intense play and kindness off the field. The hometown hero made 12 Pro Bowls in a row from 1991 to 2002.

By 2000, the Chargers had fallen to a 1–15 record. That gave them a high draft pick in 2001. They used it to select running back **LaDainian Tomlinson**. Tomlinson became one of the greatest backs in NFL history. In 2006, he was named Most Valuable Player (MVP). He recorded 1,815 rushing yards and 31 touchdowns that season.

Tight end **Antonio Gates** didn't even play football in college. He'd been a basketball player. Gates brought his basketball skills to the football field. For example, he was great

TOMLINSON
21

at jumping up for passes. He also had good speed for such a big player. When Gates retired, he had more touchdowns than any tight end in NFL history.

Quarterback **Philip Rivers** was the leader of the team's offense. After he became the starter in 2006, Rivers never missed a game. Rivers was known for his aggressive throws and fiery personality. He spent 16 years with the Chargers. During that time, he broke most of Fouts's team records. Rivers left the Chargers after the 2019 season. When he retired, he was among the NFL's top five in career passing yards and touchdown passes.

Rivers had a great lineman blocking for him in **Kris Dielman**. Dielman wasn't even

STAN THE MAN

Dan Fouts and Philip Rivers were two of the greatest quarterbacks in team history. However, they never took the Chargers to the Super Bowl. **Stan Humphries** did what Fouts and Rivers couldn't. In the 1994 season, he led San Diego to the big game. Humphries spent six years with the Chargers. As a starter, he posted a record of 47 wins and 29 losses.

RIVERS
17

drafted out of college. And he originally played defensive line. But the Chargers made him into a four-time Pro Bowler. Dielman was known for his toughness and reliability.

Gates may have been Rivers's favorite target. But wide receiver **Keenan Allen** quickly rose up the ranks of great Chargers receivers. In 2013, Allen had 71 catches and 1,046 receiving yards. Both were team records for a rookie. Injuries slowed him down in 2015 and 2016. But Allen came back strong in 2017. That season, he had the third-most receiving yards in the NFL.

The 2017 season also marked a new era for the Chargers. They moved back to the Los Angeles area. Leading them in their new home was defensive end **Joey Bosa**. The fierce pass rusher posted double-digit sacks in three of his first four seasons. Fans hoped players like Bosa would be a part of the Chargers' first Super Bowl championship team.

BOSA

97

TIMELINE

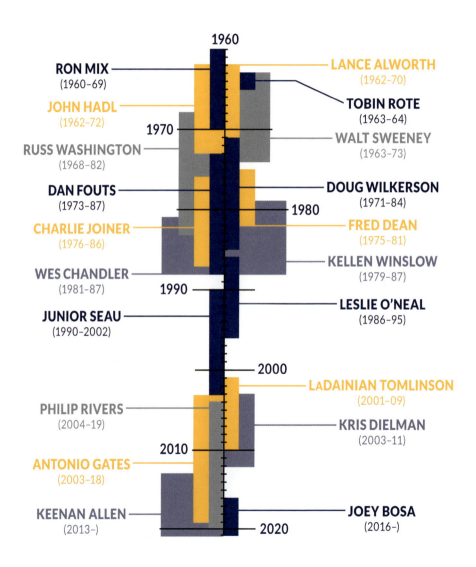

1960

RON MIX
(1960–69)

LANCE ALWORTH
(1962–70)

JOHN HADL
(1962–72)

TOBIN ROTE
(1963–64)

1970

RUSS WASHINGTON
(1968–82)

WALT SWEENEY
(1963–73)

DAN FOUTS
(1973–87)

DOUG WILKERSON
(1971–84)

1980

CHARLIE JOINER
(1976–86)

FRED DEAN
(1975–81)

KELLEN WINSLOW
(1979–87)

WES CHANDLER
(1981–87)

1990

JUNIOR SEAU
(1990–2002)

LESLIE O'NEAL
(1986–95)

2000

LaDAINIAN TOMLINSON
(2001–09)

PHILIP RIVERS
(2004–19)

KRIS DIELMAN
(2003–11)

2010

ANTONIO GATES
(2003–18)

KEENAN ALLEN
(2013–)

JOEY BOSA
(2016–)

2020

LOS ANGELES CHARGERS

Team history: Los Angeles Chargers (1960, 2017–), San Diego Chargers (1961–2016)

AFL championships: 1 (1963)

Super Bowl titles: 0*

Key coaches:

Sid Gillman (1960–69, 1971), 86–53–6, 1 AFL championship

Don Coryell (1978–86), 69–56–0

MORE INFORMATION

To learn more about the Los Angeles Chargers, go to **pressboxbooks.com/AllAccess**.

These links are routinely monitored and updated to provide the most current information available.

*1966 through 2020

GLOSSARY

draft
An event that allows teams to choose new players coming into the league.

linebacker
A player who lines up behind the defensive linemen and in front of the defensive backs.

offensive line
The players who stop defenders from reaching the quarterback and block for running backs.

Pro Bowl
The NFL's all-star game, in which the league's best players compete.

rookie
A professional athlete in his or her first year of competition.

sack
A tackle of the quarterback behind the line of scrimmage.

INDEX